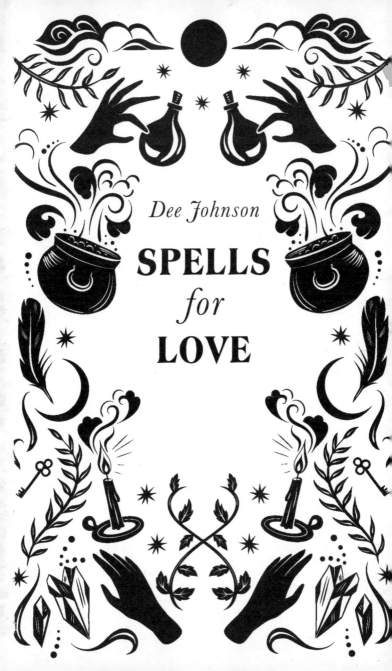

Dee Johnson

SPELLS
for
LOVE

First published in Great Britain in 2024 by

Greenfinch
An imprint of Quercus Editions Ltd
Carmelite House
50 Victoria Embankment
London EC4Y 0DZ

An Hachette UK company

A CIP catalogue record for this book is available from the British Library

HB ISBN 978-1-52943-895-6
Ebook ISBN 978-1-52943-896-3

10 9 8 7 6 5 4 3 2 1

Design by Sooky Choi
Cover design and illustrations by Holly Ovenden

Printed and bound in Great Britain by Clays Ltd, Elcograf S.p.A.

MIX
Paper | Supporting responsible forestry
FSC® C104740

Papers used by Greenfinch are from well-managed forests and other responsible sources.

Dee Johnson

SPELLS *for* LOVE

Enchantments for Relationships, Heartbreak and Romance

greenfinch

CONTENTS

INTRODUCTION

Since the beginning of time, witches have cast spells to achieve certain wishes and desires. They have studied the night sky, moon phases and planetary aspects, and they have foraged for herbs, plants and flowers. It was by combining astrological influences with botanical energies that they discovered their magick worked and was powerful.

This book features a bewitching set of love spells that expert spell-crafter and witch Dee Johnson has created. Working with these spells for her clients has brought amazing results. With this book you can explore 51 enchanting love spells, ranging a Cosmic Lover spell to a Herbal Enchantment spell. There are spells for everyone seeking to enhance their love life – spells for attracting a perfect partner, spells for strengthening an existing relationship, and spells for returning a lover who has been lost, for example.

Casting a love spell can also help to put a troubled relationship back on track, rekindling the true love you once felt for each other. Once you have the desired outcome from such a spell, it's really important that you have genuine affection and understanding, and make every effort with your relationship to make it last.

LOVE SPELL ORIGINS

The origins of love spells can be traced back to different cultures and magickal traditions – the ancient Egyptians, Greeks and Romans all created rituals aimed at enhancing love or desire. These magickal practices gradually evolved, incorporating elements from folklore, occultism and witchcraft, to result in the diverse range of love spells that are widely practised today.

History has taught us that witches have the knowledge of herbs, incantations and rituals to influence the affairs of the heart. Included in this book are little gems and secrets that Dee has been gifted through her coven work. Work with this knowledge with respect.

A fascinating aspect of witchcraft, love spells are cast to attract a special someone or to enhance an already existing relationship and can be found in various forms, from candle magick – the simplest and most popular form – to poppet magick, which is more complex.

Love spells infused with rituals and incantations are said to magickally hold the key to unlocking desires of the heart. The allure that surrounds witches and their love spells captivate those wishing to enchant their lives. The spells in this book have been created to attract love, increase passion, deepen a connection with that special someone or to reconnect with a lost love. Use them with care: love-binding spells are extremely powerful, so be sure that you really do want a lover to come back to you before casting.

CASTING A SPELL

Casting spells is an art and practice makes perfect. It can be a powerful and enlightening experience. The more spells you cast, the more confident you will feel. Witches believe in the power of spells and use them as a personal means of empowerment. You, too, can have this power. Words and thoughts hold much power – you need to believe in the magick of your spells for them to come true.

Before casting a spell, witches raise their vibration, or energy. This can be done through dance, meditation or by listening to some favourite music. Anything that 'lifts' you is a good choice. . .you are literally charging yourself up to push your spell up and out into the universe. Visualization is popular with witches: visualize a sparkling gold light flowing from the sky and into your head, right down through your body, and flowing out from your feet.

Witches are often naked (skyclad) when working with magick. This is a personal choice. If you prefer, you could wear a special dress or cloak. Be mindful to wrap up warm if you choose to cast your spell outside and it's a cold night. You don't want to be feeling uncomfortable in the middle of your spell-casting – it can be a distraction.

Casting spells requires preparation and a positive approach in order to ignite whichever spell you are performing. Organization is key. When you have worked out the best time to cast your spell, become excited about it. Liken it to a date in your diary, a special night out. This starts to build up energy. Every time you think about the event, you are adding power for a favourable outcome. Consider taking the day off work or cancelling any prior engagements to ensure that you are in a positive mind frame on the day.

Before casting your spell, make sure you will not be interrupted. Turn off your phone, set the scene, light naturally scented candles and dim the lights. Always use a lighter to light candles, and never matches, as the sulphur will kill your spell. Never blow a candle out, but always use a snuffer to extinguish it, otherwise you will blow your spell away.

A ritual bath or shower before casting a spell is important as it cleanses your body of any negative energy you might have picked up during the day. I recommend using a naturally scented bath or shower wash. Your local health food shop will have a good selection.

Spells should come directly from your heart, with positive thoughts only. After a spell has been cast, it's really important not to speak about it as this can weaken or break it. Other people's opinions might not align with yours and negative words from a friend could put doubt into your mind, so it's best to avoid this. Keeping your spell to yourself keeps it pure and strong.

INTENSIFY YOUR POWER

To add extra power to a spell, create an energy ball before casting. Place your hands together, palms cupped and slightly parted. Visualize an electric blue ball between your hands. Shape it into an energy ball of power to assist you in your spell work. When you feel ready, gently push the ball into your solar plexus. This will boost your energy for your spell work.

THE WITCH'S STORE CUPBOARD

The spells in this book are simple and easy to follow – perfect for both a beginner and an advanced practitioner of the arts – and have been created using the following accessible ingredients. Beeswax candles are great if you can source them, otherwise small spell candles are easily found online.

- Cauldron/heatproof dish
- Wand/small branch from a tree
- Coloured spell candles with holders
- Tealights
- Lighter
- Essential oils, including rose, ylang ylang, jasmine, almond, pine and patchouli
- Herbs and spices, including cinnamon, lavender, basil, bay, sage, mistletoe, chamomile, yarrow and myrtle
- Sage smudge sticks
- Incense sticks
- Crystals, including rose quartz, citrine, clear quartz, carnelian and moldavite
- Tarot cards
- Red ribbon

THE TIMING OF A LOVE SPELL

Timing is important. As a rule, love spells cast on a new moon phase are to attract new love, love spells cast on a waxing moon are to bring love closer to you and spells cast on a waning moon are to push away or banish something that no longer serves you well. Casting a love spell on a full moon creates a truly powerful spell, as this is the most magickal time of the month.

One of the best days on which to cast a love spell is a Friday, either before a full moon or on the full moon. Friday is named after the Norse goddess Freya, who represents blessings, love and lust. The day is also governed by the Roman goddess Venus, who is associated with love and fertility. The Greek goddess Aphrodite is also associated with love spells. She governs love and beauty and presides over marriage. Casting a love spell on a Friday nearest to the full moon captures the power of these goddesses, while the power of the full moon itself creates the most intense and bewitching of spells. Always take care to invoke love goddesses wisely as they are truly influential deities in relation to spells.

CREATING A LOVE ALTAR

An altar is a great way to enhance your magickal workings as having a permanent space dedicated to love can help amplify your spell-casting. Set one up on a coffee table or a windowsill – or even outside – whatever feels like the right place for you.

- Having found your space, squeeze some lemon juice and mix it with water to cleanse the surface of your altar. A toxin-free cleaner works well, too.

- Add things to make your altar special and unique to you and include candles, roses, rose quartz crystals and a picture of the person you wish to attract.

CAUTION

Never leave candles unattended. Ingredients used in this book are not intended for consumption and should not be consumed for any reason. Be aware of any ingredients you may be sensitive to and patch test on a small area. Do not use if irritation occurs. By going ahead with your spell work, you agree that this book is not responsible for any skin irritation or sensitivity while using these ingredients.

CASTING A SACRED CIRCLE

A circle creates a protective place in which to create magick. It makes a space that takes you out of the mundane world and into a protected, energized bubble, to cast spells. Here is one of many ways to cast a sacred circle in which to work your magick.

- Clear a space for your circle. Taking four candles, place one in the North of the circle, one in the East, one in the South and one in the West. Walking clockwise around the circle, light each candle in turn, sprinkling some salt as you walk from one candle to the next, to create a boundary for your circle.

- Facing North, point your finger or wand to the floor and say: 'Guardians of the North, element of earth, I bid you hail and welcome.' Now face East, keeping your finger or wand pointing to the floor, and say: 'Guardians of the East, element of air, I bid you hail and welcome.' Face South, keeping your finger or wand pointing to the floor, and say: 'Guardians of the South, element of fire, I bid you hail and welcome.' Face West, keeping your finger or wand pointing to the floor, and say: 'Guardians of the West, element of water, I bid you hail and welcome.'

- Face North again and point your finger or wand above your head. In a clockwise motion, cast your circle, starting above your head and bringing your finger or wand down to the right, then back up to the left to finish above your head again. You can now start your spell.

- When you have finished your spell, simply walk out of the circle to break it, effectively bringing its power to an end.

HOW TO MAKE MOON WATER

Moon water infuses a spell with an extra touch of magick. Use it in your rituals, add some to your ritual bath or drink some before casting a spell.

- Select a clean glass jar and fill it with water – spring water is ideal. Hold the jar and set positive intentions. If you intend to drink the moon water, cover the jar with a lid.

- Place the jar outside or on a windowsill where it can be exposed to the moonlight, preferably on a full moon. Allow the moonlight to penetrate the water.

- Collect the water at dawn to capture the moon's energy. You can store the moon water in the fridge for up to three days.

HARNESSING THE POWER OF A FULL MOON

Before starting a spell, use your hands to create a triangle by placing the tips of your index fingers together and placing your thumb tips together. Hold your hands up to the night sky and gaze at the moon through the triangle you have made. After a few moments, close your eyes, still seeing a vision of the moon. Bring the triangle down and place it up against your solar plexus, thus harnessing the moon's energy.

the
SPELLS

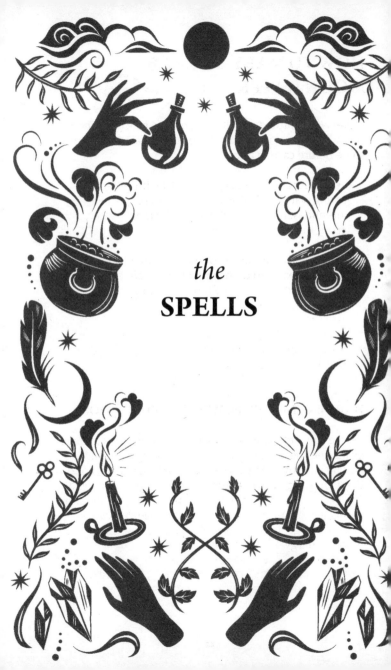

1

BLOSSOMING ROSEBUD

Cast this spell for new love on a Friday on, or before, a full moon. The mesmerizing flame of the candle will amplify your wishes. Before starting, spend time quieting your mind by way of gentle meditation.

MAGICKAL CORRESPONDENCES

- Red candle in a holder
- Lighter
- Red rose
- Small vase with water

Light the candle while holding the rose stem close to your heart, then say the following magickal words:

Gentle moonlit night,
I cast this spell tonight,
To bring fourth new love to me.
This power I claim,
So mote it be.

Repeat the words three times, using more passion each time you say it. Look deep into the candle flame and visualize your heart's true desires. Allow the candle to burn right down. Place the rose in the vase of water to seal your love spell and leave it overnight on a windowsill. In the morning, pour the water away and bury the rose with any remaining candle wax in a plant pot or in a special place in your garden.

2

APHRODITE LOVE BAG

Cast this spell of attraction on a full moon. Before starting, determine your intent and visualize the outcome you desire. You may use an already sewn bag or make your bag from scratch. Red and pink bags inspire passion and love. Cleanse your area before casting your spell. You can do this using incense or sage.

* * *

MAGICKAL CORRESPONDENCES

- Rose oil
- Ylang ylang oil
- Rose quartz crystal
- Seashell
- Red or pink satin bag

Sprinkle a few drops of both oils onto the crystal and hold it in your left hand. With your right hand, place the seashell next to your heart and repeat the following magickal words three times:

Powers above and powers below,
In perfect harmony love will flow.
With your help from above,
Aphrodite bless me with true love.
This is my wish,
So mote it be.

Whenever you meet the person you are attracted to, hold the crystal to enchant them. Keep the crystal in the satin bag and carry it around in your purse or handbag to attract your true love.

3

TAROT SOULMATE

Cast this spell of attraction on a waxing moon phase, on a Friday night closest to a full moon. The Two of Cups is the 'soul mate' card in the tarot deck. Using it here will boost the spell's energy.

MAGICKAL CORRESPONDENCES

- Red candle in a holder
- Lighter
- 2 rose quartz crystals
- Two of Cups tarot card

Light the candle and hold the crystals in your hand. Place the tarot card next to the candle. Focus on the candle for a moment, then say the following magickal words:

Lord and lady shining bright,
Fill my heart with love and light.
Red candle burns with passion and fire,
Bring forth my heart's true desire.
So mote it be.

Allow the candle to burn right down, then place the tarot card and one of the crystals under your pillow and keep them there until you have connected with your soulmate. Bury the other crystal with the remaining candle wax under a rose bush in the garden.

4

COSMIC LOVERS

Cast this spell of attraction on a new moon. Using a tarot card in your love spell can enhance its energy. The Lovers card symbolizes balance, love and harmony. When casting this spell, visualize the type of person you wish to attract.

MAGICKAL CORRESPONDENCES

- Red candle in a holder or tealight
- Lighter
- 2 rose quartz crystals
- The Lovers tarot card

Light the candle and then place the two crystals on The Lovers card. Stare into the flame and say the following magickal words:

I see you, I feel you.
We are now one,
Lover come to me.
The spell is now done,
So mote it be.

Allow the candle to burn down. Place one crystal under your pillow and bury the other crystal with any remaining wax under a rose bush in your garden.

5

GODDESS FREYA LOVE SPELL

Cast this spell of attraction on a new moon. Magick starts from within, from love for ourselves to love from another. The process of casting a spell is beautiful and sacred and this simple and easy love spell is perfect for a beginner. It will help to attract 'the one' if you're tired of looking for that special someone or have your eye on a person that you would like to entice into your life.

MAGICKAL CORRESPONDENCES

- Cocktail stick
- Red candle in a holder
- Lighter

Use the cocktail stick to etch your name into the candle and the words 'love come to me'. Light the candle and say the following magickal words:

Powers above and powers below,
I ask for love to magickally flow
Forever in perfect harmony.
Grant my wish,
So mote it be.

Allow the candle to burn down. When the wax has cooled but is still soft, etch the rune symbol associated with the goddess Freya into the wax. Called gebu, the symbol simply looks like an X and represents love and partnership. Bury the remaining wax under a laurel bush in your garden.

6

GODDESS FREYA MAGICKAL POUCH

Cast this spell of attraction on a Friday, on a waxing moon phase. Friday is named after the goddess Freya, who governs love. Work with her to allow her magickal essence to infuse your love spell.

MAGICKAL CORRESPONDENCES

- Red candle in a holder
- Rose oil
- Almond oil
- Lighter
- 2 red roses
- Rose quartz crystal
- Red or pink silk pouch

Anoint the candle with a drop of rose oil mixed with a drop of almond oil and avoiding the wick. Light the candle, then place the roses behind the candle. While holding the crystal, say the following magickal words:

Goddess Freya of the night sky,
Shine your light on me.
Passion and love,
Your gift from above,
My heart is open,
So mote it be.

Allow the candle to burn right down, then place the petals from the roses in the silk pouch with the rose quartz crystal. At night, hold the pouch for a few moments to absorb Freya's energy and connect to the love energy it holds. Within a moon cycle (one month) you should have attracted a new romantic interest.

Witchy Tip

Always work in a clockwise (deosil) direction when you anoint a candle, as this will attract energy to you. Anointing a candle in an anti-clockwise (widdershins) direction will repel or push away energy from you.

7

SWEETHEART BATH SACHET

Cast this spell of attraction as you take a bath on a Friday on a waxing moon phase. It will add a touch of love and enchantment to your self-care routine.

MAGICKAL CORRESPONDENCES

- Small muslin bag
- Dried rose petals
- Dried jasmine flowers
- Dried lavender
- 2 red tealights
- Lighter
- Fresh pink and red rose petals
- Rose quartz crystal

Place equal measures of the dried flowers in the muslin bag and tie the top. Place the bag in your warm bath water. As the water becomes infused with the essence of these elements, visualize love flowing into your life. Light the red tealights and scatter the fresh rose petals around your bath. As you lie in your bath, hold the crystal close to your heart and say the following magickal words:

As I lovingly infuse my skin,
Allowing sacred love to flow in,
Element of water, love flows to me.
This ritual is cast,
So mote it be.

Allow the candles to burn right down as you relax in your magickal bath, connecting to the love energy it holds. Repeat once a week for a moon cycle (one month), or until you have you attracted a new romantic interest.

8
WISH UPON A MOON

Cast this love energy spell on a full moon. The full moon has amazing influence and is a powerful time to cast a love spell. Witches are well known to work with the moon's power at this time. Enjoy the magick of this special night.

MAGICKAL CORRESPONDENCES

- White candle in a holder or tealight
- Lighter
- Jasmine petals
- Rose petals
- Clear quartz crystal
- Small bowl

Light the candle and hold the petals and crystal in your hands. Close your eyes and feel loving energy flow through you into the petals and crystal. Say the following magickal words while staring into the flame:

By the light of the silver moon,
Love blossoms and blooms.
With petals of jasmine and petals of rose,
Loves energy gently flows.
As I will,
So mote it be.

Place the crystal and the petals in a small bowl and bury them with any remaining candle wax in a special place in your garden or in a woodland.

9

WELCOMING LOVE

Cast this spell on a waxing or full moon phase to attract new love.

MAGICKAL CORRESPONDENCES

- Mortar and pestle
- Almond oil
- Rose oil
- Fresh mint
- Fresh sage
- Red candle in a holder
- Lighter

Combine a few drops of almond oil with one drop of rose oil in the mortar and add a sprig of mint and a pinch of sage. Use the pestle to stir the ingredients three times in a clockwise direction, then anoint the candle from top to bottom, avoiding the wick. Light the candle and say the following magickal words:

I conjure a new love
With blessings from above.
Love and passion, this I seek,
Bring me my love
Forever to keep.
This is my wish,
So mote it be.

Once the candle has burned down, bury the remaining wax outside your front door to welcome in new love.

10

SPARKLING STAR COMMUNICATION

Use this spell to ignite communication with your loved one and to bring a spark back into your relationship. Cast the spell on a Wednesday, which is governed by Mercury the planet of communication, and on a waxing moon phase.

MAGICKAL CORRESPONDENCES

- Orange candle in a holder
- Lighter
- White or orange paper
- Red pen
- Heatproof dish
- Photograph of a star constellation
- Biodegradable silver glitter

Light the candle, then write the name of the person you want to have communication with on a piece of paper. Light the paper and let it burn in the dish. Gaze at the photo of the stars, sprinkle the glitter around the candle and whisper the following sweet magickal words:

Under the moon's silver gentle glow,
Love's enchantment shall forever flow.
As the candlelight flickers

And the stars sparkle and glitter,
Our entwined hearts shall forever flow.
So mote it be.

Snuff out the candle. Step outside with the dish and blow the ashes of the paper with any remaining glitter to the wind under the twinkling stars.

11

MAGICKAL RIVER SPELL

Cast this spell of true love on a Friday, on a waxing moon phase. Water is, by its nature, cleansing and healing. It represents our emotions and when something is important to us, this is when we are emotionally connected. Water is essential to life – from each drop of rain from the sky to the water we bathe or shower in. This water spell is highly connected to our emotions and can be performed by a stream, river or lake.

MAGICKAL CORRESPONDENCES

- Red rose petals
- River or moving water

Holding the petals in your hands, visualize the qualities of the type of person you want to attract, and say the following magickal words:

Element of water that flows through the earth,
Power of the universe, this is my worth.
With these petals this spell I cast,
True love is mine that will forever last.
As I will,
So mote it be.

When you are ready, gently throw the petals into the river. Sit and connect with the earth and listen to the sweet sound of the water as it flows gently by. The universe hears your wishes and your words.

12

ZODIAC LOVE

Cast this binding love spell on a full moon. Our zodiac sign is the heart and core of who we are. We are connected to this sign from the moment we are born into the universe and for all our time on earth. The energy of this spell divinely connects two souls together as one, simply by using both your full names, dates of birth and zodiac signs.

MAGICKAL CORRESPONDENCES

- Cocktail stick
- 2 red candles in holders
- String
- Ground cinnamon
- Rosemary leaves
- Lighter

Clear a special and peaceful space for this spell and cast a sacred circle of protection around you (see page 13). Use the cocktail stick to carve the person of interest's name, date of birth and zodiac sign into one candle. Carve your own name, date of birth and zodiac sign into the other candle. Tie the two candles together and sprinkle cinnamon and rosemary around the bottom. Light the candles and say your spell aloud while visualizing the love you desire. Say the following magickal words three times:

Almighty goddess on this night,
Bind (name of person) to me.
Two souls have now become one.
So mote it be.

Allow the candles to burn right down and bury any remaining ingredients including the candle wax in a place that reminds you of your person of interest.

13

A POTENT LOVE HONEY JAR

Cast this spell on a Friday before a new noon.
A gift from the bee nation, honey is a sacred ingredient. This sweet elixir has been used in magick as both food and medicine since ancient times. Use this magickal honey jar spell to make your life sweeter and to sweeten someone's feelings towards you, attracting love and romance.

MAGICKAL CORRESPONDENCES

- Pink or red candle in a holder
- Lighter
- Glass jar
- Dried rose petals/buds
- Honey
- Lavender oil
- Chilli flakes

Light your candle and gently place the rose petals/buds and a little honey in the jar. Add three drops of lavender oil and a sprinkling of chilli flakes. Holding the jar close to your heart, think of the person you want to attract and say the following magickal words:

Divine powers that we can't see,
Bless this union, forever are we.
Bonds of romance we shall bind,
Always forever in love entwined.
So mote it be.

Keep the jar somewhere special in your bedroom and wait for your spell to come true.

14

MAGICKAL MARRIAGE COMMITMENT

Cast this spell of commitment on a full moon. With a dash of magick those four words: 'Will you marry me' can be made to happen. The union of two people coming together closer than ever before lies in this spell.

MAGICKAL CORRESPONDENCES

- Photo featuring both parties
- Parchment paper
- Red pen
- Rose oil
- Heatproof dish

Place the photo on a table in front of you. On a piece of parchment paper, write your lover's name three times, then write your name three times over theirs. Draw a circle clockwise three times around the names and add a drop of rose oil. Fold the piece of paper three times towards you. Burn the paper in a heatproof dish to seal your spell. Say the following magickal words with passion and fire as the paper burns:

By the power of the cosmos and the energy of true love,
I summon the forces below,
I summon the forces above.
Our love is strong, pure and true,
Everlasting in all we do.
Marriage, happiness and love I manifest,
With grace we are now and forever blessed.
So mote it be.

Bury any remaining ashes under a rose bush in your garden and await your loved one to get down on one knee.

15

GODDESS VENUS FRUITY LOVE

Cast this spell on the Friday before a full moon. The magickal and feminine properties of grapes come under the zodiac of Taurus. This Earth sign symbolizes the finer things in life. Connected to the third-eye and root chakras, this fruit will transform your life spiritually.

MAGICKAL CORRESPONDENCES

- Cocktail stick
- Red candle
- Soil
- Heatproof dish
- Lighter
- Red grapes
- Carnelian crystal

Use the cocktail stick to carve your lover's name into the candle. Place some soil in the heatproof dish and stand the candle in the soil. Light the candle, close your eyes and envision the person as you say the following words:

The vine it binds, we are one.
Our hearts entwine, you are mine.
Desire and fire bound in bliss,
Sealed with love's eternal kiss.

Together forever united as one.
I cast this spell,
Now it has been done.
So mote it be.

Eat some of the grapes while envisioning your lover. Once the candle goes out, take any remains and bury them in a place that reminds you of them. Leave a carnelian crystal on top to give thanks to the universe for this spell.

16

LOVE POPPET

Cast this spell on a Friday before a full moon. In magick, a poppet spell uses a doll to represent a person for a magickal purpose. Create a bond between the doll and yourself before casting the spell and cast a sacred circle *(see page 13)* *once ready to go ahead.*

MAGICKAL CORRESPONDENCES

- Red cloth
- Scissors
- Needle and red thread
- Rose petals
- Rose quartz crystal
- Ylang ylang oil
- Picture of the person you wish to attract
- Pen
- Red silk scarf

Begin by cutting a poppet from the red cloth (two pieces) and sew the poppet together leaving a gap. (You may wish to purchase a ready-made poppet online.) Fill the poppet with the rose petals, crystal and one drop of ylang ylang oil. Finish by placing the picture of the person inside the poppet and sew it up. You can decorate the poppet to personalize it further – for example, write your lover's initials on the front or draw a face.

Once you have created your sacred circle, hold the poppet next to your heart and say the following magickal words:

This poppet represents my desire.
Our love will never tire.
Love's gentle touch embrace,
Blessed with love and grace.
So mote it be.

Close your eyes and hold the poppet close to your chest, connecting your two hearts. When finished, wrap the poppet in a red silk scarf and keep it safe in a drawer in your bedroom.

17

ROSE WATER JAR

Cast this spell of wish fulfilment on a new moon. Roses have long been associated with love spells and are well established as enhancers of any type of love spell. We give roses as a sign of our love.

MAGICKAL CORRESPONDENCES

- Glass jar
- Rosehips
- Rosebuds
- Ground cinnamon
- Chilli flakes
- Rose quartz crystal
- Rose water
- White paper
- Red pen
- Red candle in a holder
- Lighter

Place one or two rosehips and rosebuds in the jar with a pinch each of ground cinnamon and chilli flakes. Add the crystal and some rose water. Write your name on a piece of paper three times, each one below the one before it. On the other side of the paper, write what you want your lover to look like and be like – for example, with blue eyes, kind and loving – be very specific.

This candle burns a flame of fire,
Bring forth my heart's true desire.
As I will,
So mote it be.

Allow the candle to burn right down, until the water extinguishes it. Bury the remaining wax in a special place close to your home and pour any remaining water over the top. Cast this spell once a week for three weeks.

19

YULETIDE MISTLETOE LOVE BOTTLE

Cast this spell of attraction on 21 December. Mistletoe has long been associated as a herb of love and protection. For ancient druids, it was the most sacred of herbs for its magickal qualities.

MAGICKAL CORRESPONDENCES

- Red candle in a holder
- Lighter
- White paper
- Red pen
- Red ribbon
- Small glass bottle
- Dried or fresh mistletoe
- Hibiscus flowers
- Rose petals and buds

Light the candle, then write your name and date of birth on a piece of paper. In just a few words, write down the type of lover you want to attract. Roll the paper towards you, like a scroll, then tie the ribbon around it. Pour a little candle wax onto the ribbon to seal it, then place it in the bottle. Sprinkle the mistletoe and flowers on top and put on the lid. Pour some wax onto the lid to seal it and say the following magickal words while holding the bottle.

With blessings from above,
Love and passion, this I seek.
Bring me my love, forever to keep.
With this flame, it burns so bright,
These words I chant into the night.
So mote it be.

Allow the candle to burn right down and bury any remaining ingredients under a favourite plant in your garden. Keep the bottle in a place that is special to you.

20

VALENTINE'S SOULMATE

Cast this spell on Valentine's Day. February 14 has long been associated with love. Harness the power on this special day with this love spell. If the moon is visible through a window allow her rays to illuminate the room you are casting your spell in.

MAGICKAL CORRESPONDENCES

- Extra-virgin olive oil
- Rose oil
- Vanilla oil
- Ground cinnamon
- Red candle in a holder
- Lighter

Mix a teaspoon of olive oil with a drop each of rose and vanilla oil and some cinnamon. Use the mix to anoint the candle, avoiding the wick. Light the candle, hold it and charge it by saying the following magickal words:

Candle of magick,
Enchant this spell.
Bring me my soulmate to love me well.
I conjure my love,
With blessings from above,
Love and passion, this I seek.

Bring me my soulmate forever to keep.
With this flame, it burns so bright,
These words I chant into this special night.
So mote it be.

Allow the candle to burn right down and bury any remaining ingredients under a special plant in your garden or close to your home.

21

LOVE IS AT BAY

Cast this spell for eternal love on a Friday, on a starry night with a waxing moon. Bay leaves have long been known to attract love. They are a symbol of power, bringing life to any love spell.

* * *

MAGICKAL CORRESPONDENCES

- Red candle in a holder
- Lighter
- 3 bay leaves
- Red pen
- Heatproof dish

Light the candle. Write the word 'love' on one of the bay leaves, then light the leaf in the flame and place it in the heatproof dish to burn. Say the following magickal words:

Goddess Venus, hear this spell I cast,
For a sweet eternal love that will last.
As the shining stars above brightly glow,
Beautiful Venus let love flow.
This spell is cast,
Love comes to me fast.
So mote it be.

Let the candle burn down and bury the wax and any remaining ashes in a pot plant or in a special place in your garden. Sleep with the other two bay leaves under your pillow to help enhance the love energy of the spell. Repeat this spell regularly until you have found new love.

22

BELTANE MARRIAGE BINDER

Cast this spell on 1 May. The feast of Beltane has long been associated with marriage and commitment. It marks the midway point between the spring equinox and the summer solstice.

MAGICKAL CORRESPONDENCES

- Cocktail stick
- 2 red candles in holders
- Almond oil
- Yang ylang oil
- Rose oil
- Red rose petals
- Ground cinnamon
- Dried chamomile leaves
- Heatproof dish
- String
- Lighter

Use the cocktail stick to carve the person of interest's name and date of birth into one candle. Carve your own name and date of birth into the other candle. Mix together a teaspoon of almond oil with a drop each of ylang ylang and rose oil and use this to anoint the candles, avoiding the wicks. Stand the candles in their holders in the heatproof dish and sprinkle rose petals, cinnamon and dried chamomile leaves around their bases. Tie the candles together with string. Light the candles and say the following magickal words:

Silver moon on this enchanting night,
Bind this love with all your might.
Let love be ours for eternity.
As I will,
So mote it be.

Allow the candles to burn right down together. Bury the wax and any remaining ingredients under a tree in a special place in a forest or the woods.

23

SUMMER SOLSTICE TYING THE KNOT

Cast this spell of marriage and commitment on 21 June. Summer Solstice, or Litha, is when the sun's energy is at its pinnacle and magickal energy is at its fullest. This is a most magickal time to cast a love spell. Decorating your altar or special place with sunflowers will add an extra touch of magick to this spell. Cleanse your area before casting your spell. You can do this using incense or sage.

MAGICKAL CORRESPONDENCES

- A ring of any kind that fits the marriage finger (left hand, fourth finger)
- Red or pink ribbon

Visualizing what you want from your spell, thread the ribbon through the ring, then hold both ends of the ribbon together with the ring hanging in the middle. Slowly and steadily, tie nine knots along the length of the ribbon, starting at the ring and working towards the loose ends. With each knot, say a line of the following words:

Ribbon knot one, the spell has begun.
Ribbon knot two, this spell shall come true.
Ribbon knot three, we are meant to be.
Ribbon knot four, a love like never before.

Ribbon knot five, our love will thrive.
Ribbon knot six, with this enchanting mix.
Ribbon knot seven, this spell I beckon.
Ribbon knot eight, this is our fate.
Ribbon knot nine, now is our time.

Your intent is very important with each knot you tie. Once all the knots are tied, keep the ring with the ribbon close to you until the spell has come to fruition.

24

POWERFUL HONEY JAR

Cast this spell of wish fulfilment on a new moon. Honey is a sacred ingredient and harnessing its power will help you live a sweeter, more magickal life full of love. There is a long history of folk magick traditions that work with honey or sugar to attract love. Good options for vegans are vegan sugar and maple syrup. This spell will allow you to bring sweet love into your life – it is a great example of sympathetic magick, where like attracts like.

MAGICKAL CORRESPONDENCES

- White candle in a holder
- Lighter
- White paper
- Red pen
- Glass jar
- Vanilla essence
- Dried rosemary
- Ground ginger
- Ground cinnamon
- Honey

Light the candle. Write what it is that you would like sweetened in your love life on a piece of paper. Place the paper in the jar with a teaspoon of vanilla essence and a pinch each of the herbs and spices. Then pour a little honey on top. Close the jar and seal it with the wax from the candle, dripping wax all along where the lid meets the glass until completely sealed.

Put your hands around the jar and visualize what it is you want. Stare into the candle flame and gently say: 'This is the flame of my desire, this is the flame of my desire, this is the flame of my desire.' Let your voice grow louder with each repeat. Finish your spell by saying: So mote it be.

Keep the honey jar in a special place until your spell comes true.

25

CRYSTAL REUNION

Cast this spell of reunion on a Friday, on a waxing moon. Before you do so, make sure you are truly ready to reconnect with your ex as this spell works quickly. Keep your work confidential as speaking about your magickal work can weaken its effects.

MAGICKAL CORRESPONDENCES

- Cocktail stick
- 2 red candles in holders
- Honey
- Heatproof plate
- String
- Photo of you and your ex
- Lighter
- Brown sugar
- Rose quartz crystal

Use a cocktail stick to carve your ex's full name and date of birth into one candle and your full name and date of birth into the other candle. Anoint the candles with a little honey, avoiding the wicks, and place them in their candle holders on the heatproof plate, then tie them with string. Place the photo in a safe place behind the candles. Light the candles and, staring into the flame, visualize a time when you and your ex were happy together.

Sprinkle some brown sugar around the candles to make things sweeter between you both, then say the following words. Start with a whisper and grow louder each time you say them. Be sure to put all your energy into the words and keep visualizing the two of you together.

Whispering words of love, magick and true,
This spell shall reclaim me and you.
With moonlight passion and magick so bright,
I cast this spell, our love will reignite.
So mote it be.

Allow the candles to burn down with the photo in the background and then bury the remainder of the wax in the earth. Leave a rose quartz crystal to give thanks.

Witchy Tip
The more you stare into the flame as you visualize your intentions, the more effective, your spell will be.

26

FROM FRIEND TO LOVER

Cast this spell on a new moon. Pink candle magick represents gentle and compassionate love without the sexual undertones implied with red. Pink candles are the candles of romance and sweet tender love. They bring powerful and gentle energies that can attract a long-lasting relationship or nurture a friendship into something more. Pink is associated with the heart chakra and is a healing colour that warms and works to bring togetherness and gentle change.

MAGICKAL CORRESPONDENCES

- Extra-virgin olive oil
- Small bowl
- Rosewood oil
- Peppermint oil
- Ground cinnamon
- Pink candle in a holder
- Lighter

Place a teaspoon of extra-virgin olive oil in a small bowl and add one drop of rosewood oil, one drop of peppermint oil and a sprinkling of cinnamon. Combine the mixture and use your fingertips to anoint the candle, avoiding the wick. As you do this, envision what you would like to happen. When ready, light the candle and say the following magickal words:

Goddess, Goddess, high above,
Turn friendship into true love.
(Name of person) is deeply in love with me.
This spell is cast,
So mote it be.

Let the candle burn down; keep your energy focused and meditate gently while the magick works. Bury the remaining wax in your front garden – it will be activated when your friend walks in this space, bringing the love you desire.

27

BIRTHDAY LOVE CANDLE

Cast this spell of wish fulfilment on your birthday. This is your special day – a day of celebration and a little extra magick. You will have heard of making a wish on your birthday and blowing out a candle on your cake. . .it was once said that when the candles went out the wishes were released to the moon goddess.

MAGICKAL CORRESPONDENCES

- A cupcake of your choice
- White birthday candle in a holder
- Rose petals
- Lighter

Stand the candle in its holder in the cake. Sprinkle some rose petals around the cake. Light the candle and say the following magickal words:

Moonlight beams and starry night skies,
Bring love to me before my eyes.
I cast this spell on my special night,
Bring me love for my heart's delight.
So mote it be.

After saying these words, visualize your wish and with that picture in your mind, cup your hands to your mouth and blow the picture into your hands. Now, with your hands still cupped, throw your wish into the flame. Snuff the candle out when you are ready and eat and enjoy your birthday cake.

Witchy Tip

Be sure to snuff out your candle, and not blow it out, once you have made your wish. It is said to blow the candle out is to blow your wish away.

28

HALLOWEEN SPELL

To remove an obstacle standing in your way to love, cast this spell of banishment on 31 October. Halloween, or Samhain, marks the end of the old year and the start of the new one. It's the best time to banish any obstacles and is the biggest night of the year for witches. It's their New Year's Eve, a time of great magick and celebration. Halloween is a powerful time to cast spells as it is believed the veil between the living and the spirit world is at its thinnest.

MAGICKAL CORRESPONDENCES

- Red candle in a holder
- Lighter
- Black paper
- Silver pen
- Small heatproof dish
- Small glass jar
- Moon water (see page 14)
- Pine oil
- Lavender oil

Light the candle. On a piece of black paper, write at least one thing you want to release to improve your relationship. It could be fear of commitment or jealousy – whatever you feel is blocking your relationship.

Burn the paper in the small dish. Cleanse the jar and pour in some moon water and a drop each of pine and lavender oil. Stir the mix in a clockwise direction. Add the ashes from the paper, then hold the jar and say the following magickal words:

Goddess of the sky,
I call on thee
To banish any negativity
Between [name of obstacle] and I.
I bid you farewell and goodbye.
So mote it be.

Take the jar to a nearby park or woodland, dig a hole and pour the ingredients back to the earth. Cleanse the jar and recycle.

Witchy Tip
You can use the smoke from an incense stick to cleanse the jar.

29

RED RIBBON PASSION

Cast this spell of wish fulfilment on a Friday before a full moon. Witches work with red ribbons to tie something to them. Red ribbons have long been associated with love and passion – red is the colour of passion, love and deep desires. Working with red ribbons enhances a spell's energy and focuses on attracting the desired love. This spell will bring zest and sparkle back into your love life when passion is running low.

MAGICKAL CORRESPONDENCES

- Orange
- Red ribbon
- Knife
- Small bowl
- Extra-virgin olive oil
- Vanilla essence
- Ground cinnamon
- Dried basil
- Red candle
- Lighter

Tie the ribbon around the orange. As you do so, envision your lover coming back into your arms. Gently carve a hole in the top of the orange for your candle. In the bowl, combine one teaspoon of olive oil with a drop of vanilla essence, a sprinkling of cinnamon and a pinch of basil. Use the mixture to anoint the candle, avoiding the wick. Light the candle and stand it in the orange, then say the following magickal words:

Goddess Venus on this night,
Candle flame burning bright,
Bring back passion and romance
With this flickering candle's dance.
So mote it be.

Allow the candle to burn right down, then bury the remaining wax with the orange and any leftover herbs in a place that reminds you of your lover.

30

KITCHEN WITCHERY

Cast this spell on a Friday before a full moon. The spell involves making a soup to enhance feelings of affection and love. It is perfect to serve to your loved one on a cold and frosty day. Creating a love magick soup involves selecting ingredients with symbolic associations to love and passion.

MAGICKAL CORRESPONDENCES

- Cauldron or saucepan
- Knife
- Magickal soup potion ingredients (see box)
- Stock
- Salt and pepper
- White bowl

MAGICKAL SOUP POTION INGREDIENTS
Tomatoes: for passion and love
Red peppers: for sweetness and affection
Basil: for love and fertility
Rosemary: to enhance love and protection
Thyme: to attract affection and good luck
Chilli peppers: to ignite passion
Carrots: for vitality
Ginger: to add a fiery element

Infuse each ingredient with your intentions as you prepare the soup. Flavour the soup with salt and pepper as you wish, and say the following words:

With strength and sweetness balanced is thus,
within this soup, within us.

Serve in a white bowl to the person of interest.

31

LEMON LOVE

Cast this spell of attraction at midnight on a new moon. Love is the most magickal feeling in the universe. To fall in love brings us joy and happiness – it's the greatest feeling you could have in your entire life. This enchanting lemon love spell harnesses the vibrancy of this citrus fruit to attract romantic energies into your life.

MAGICKAL CORRESPONDENCES

- Lemon
- Knife
- Sugar
- Red ribbon

Begin by carving your wish into the lemon's skin and sprinkle the words with a little sugar to add sweetness. Bind the lemon with the red ribbon. As you do so, whisper sweet words of love into the fruit, infusing it with your wishes and desires. Hold the lemon close to your heart and say the following magickal words three times, becoming louder with each repeat. Visualize yourself with your lost love:

Lemon bright in the moon's gleam,
Whispered words of love,
Sweet dream.

Sugar kisses,
Sweetness profound.
Red ribbon binds, my love is now bound.
So mote it be.

Place the lemon in a special place in your home, allowing the magickal energies to radiate out. Feel your love flourishing.

32

WICCAN SPELL FOR NEW LOVE

Cast this new love spell on a Friday, on a waxing moon phase. Within the sacred circle of Wiccan practice, love spell rituals blossom. Wicca is modernized witchcraft, mixing the old ways with the new. This Wiccan spell does exactly this, combining ways of old with more modern versions of the craft to create this all-encompassing spell.

* * *

MAGICKAL CORRESPONDENCES

- Plate
- Dried oregano
- Dried chamomile
- Extra-virgin olive oil
- Rosewood oil
- • Pink candle in a holder
- Lighter

Mix a pinch of each herb with the olive oil and a drop of rosewood oil on the plate, then roll the candle in it, working in a clockwise direction and avoiding the wick. Light the candle and say the following magickal words:

Goddess Freya, I call upon your power.
I cast this spell at midnight's hour.
Beneath moonlit dance,

In Wiccan grace,
Candles flicker, love's embrace.
Herbs and crystals, spell interlace,
Whispered words in this sacred space,
Intent entwined, in nature's trance,
Wiccan magick love's dance.
So mote it.

Let the candle burn down and bury any remaining ingredients under a special tree in a wood or forest.

33

SECRET SPELL BAG FOR LOVE'S DESIRE

Cast this spell of enchantment on a waxing moon phase. Within this love spell, a magickal mixture of romantic energies combines: rose petals symbolize passion and the sweet lavender, attraction. The rose quartz is a crystal that harbours desires. Cinnamon sticks spark passion's flame, while a handwritten note seals intentions. This carefully crafted pouch becomes a creation of enchantment, a tangible manifestation of yearning. As it rests closed, its energy resonates with the heart's desires, creating a magnetic allure. The love spell bag is a mystick fusion of herbs and crystals and transmits amorous wishes to the universe.

MAGICKAL CORRESPONDENCES

- Red candle in a holder
- Lighter
- Red silk pouch
- 2 rose quartz crystals
- Cinnamon stick
- Rose petals
- Patchouli oil
- Lavender oil

Light the candle. Place the two crystals in the pouch with the rose petals, cinnamon stick and a drop each of lavender and patchouli oil. Hold the spell bag and say the following magickal words:

In this bag of love, petals and rhyme,
Rose quartz glows, a love sublime.
Cinnamon's warmth, passion's chime,
A dance of desires, in rhythm and rhyme.
So mote it be.

Keep the spell bag somewhere safe until you have found a new love.

34

HERBAL ENCHANTMENT

Cast this love spell on a full moon. This herbal spell combines truly magickal ingredients to create a powerful botanical spell. Work with organic ingredients where possible for extra potency. The use of lavender in your love spell enhances soft feelings of affection and endearment. Cinnamon evokes passion and the mystery of a seductive romance and orris root is well known for its ability to draw love to you. Orris root is also governed by the moon, which gives it that extra mystery element.

MAGICKAL CORRESPONDENCES

- Small bowl
- Dried basil
- Dried rose
- Dried lavender
- Ground cinnamon
- Orris root powder
- Red silk pouch

In the bowl, mix together a teaspoon each of the magickal basil, rose and lavender with a pinch each of cinnamon and orris root. As you stir, visualize the love you seek with intense passion. Hold the pouch and say the following magickal words:

Basil for passion, rose for love's delight,
Lavender whispers in the enchanting night.
Cinnamon's warmth a magickal blend,
Passion and love to the universe I send.
So mote it be.

Keep your magickal herbal pouch with you. Blow a little of the herbal mix onto your next lover to keep passion and romance alive.

35

APPLE LOVE

Cast this powerful and enchanting spell of everlasting love on a Friday and on a full moon. Apples have a long and magickal history. Traditionally a forbidden fruit, the apple also has connections to the ancient Greek goddesses Aphrodite and Gaia. It symbolizes eternal love and abundance. In folklore, apples are associated with divination, opening the gates to the underworld and eternal life.

MAGICKAL CORRESPONDENCES

- Red apple
- Knife
- Spoon or scoop
- Lavender oil
- Dried chamomile
- Fresh red, pink or white rose petals
- Honey
- Small clear quartz crystals
- Small citrine crystals
- White paper
- Red pen
- Needle and red thread
- Cocktail stick
- 2 red candles in holders
- Lighter

Cut the top off the apple and scoop out the inside using a spoon or scoop. Into the hole, add three drops of lavender oil, a sprinkle of chamomile, the rose petals and a teaspoon of honey. Next, add the crystals. Write your lover's name and date of birth on one piece of paper, then write your name and date of birth on another. Fold each piece of paper three times towards you and place inside the hole. Sew the apple together. Use the cocktail stick to etch each of your names on a candle, then place the candles either side of the apple and light them. Say the following magickal words three times:

You are the apple of my eye,
Love me forever til I die.
Two souls are forever entwined,
A love forever that is yours, ours and mine.
So mote it be.

Visualize both of you together, happy and in love, while the candles burn down to the bottom. When the candles have both burned down, take the apple and bury it in a special place in the earth. Sprinkle any remaining wax, herbs and petals over the spot.

36

'A' IS FOR 'APPLE'

Cast this spell of enchantment on a full moon. This is an easy and effective apple love spell to enchant your loved one. The apple has long been regarded as the symbol of desire and this simple spell will have your lover swooped off their feet in no time.

MAGICKAL CORRESPONDENCES

- Shiny red apple
- Knife
- Plate
- Ground cinnamon
- Honey, agave syrup or maple syrup
- Peanut butter (optional)

Slowly peel and core the apple. As you do so, say the following magickal words while visualizing your intent:

A as above,
Bring me my love.
As I call high
To the Goddess in the sky.
All is divine,
You are now mine.
So mote it be.

Give the apple a wash, cleansing its energy. Chop the apple, place it on the plate and add a sprinkling of cinnamon and a drizzle of honey or syrup. Add some peanut butter if you desire. As you eat each slice you can choose to repeat the above incantation in your mind or out loud. As you do, visualize a warm, pink glow of love and abundance in your body. Be sure to thank the goddesses for the blessings you have now received.

Witchy Tip

If you happen to be seeing the person your heart desires, offer them a slice. It is said that apples represent the human heart, so connecting your hearts by lovingly sharing will ensure you enjoy a romantic future together.

37

THREE OF CUPS LOVE

Cast this spell of wish fulfilment on a Friday, on a full moon. The meaning behind the Three of Cups in tarot is happiness and celebration. It can also indicate a happy reunion with a loved one. A tarot card can be a powerful tool in a spell, especially when combined with other magickal ingredients.

MAGICKAL CORRESPONDENCES

- Three of Cups tarot card
- Red candle in a holder
- Lighter
- Pink rose petals
- Wand

Hold the Three of Cups in your hands and visualize the happiness and love that you wish for. Allow the energy of the card to flow through you. Set your space, lighting the candle and laying two rose petals on each side of the tarot card. Sprinkle the remaining the rose petals around the card, three times, to make a heart-shaped circle. As you do so, say the following magickal words:

A love spell passionately unfurls,
Roses bloom, their essence swirls,
Words woven like silk, a spell-binding rite,

Eternal enchantment, pure and bright.
So mote it be.

As your love spell unfolds, cast a magick circle with the wand, working in a clockwise direction. Visualize what it is you are wanting and stop when feel you have manifested your heart's desire. Allow the candle to burn down as the pink petals weave their magick and your spell of true love is cast. Bury any remaining ingredients under a rose bush in your garden.

38

GODDESS HECATE MAGICK MIRROR

Cast this spell of wish fulfilment on the Friday nearest to a full moon. Hecate was the powerful ancient Greek goddess presiding over magick, spells and the night moon. Her name means 'worker from afar'; casting this spell will harness her powers and she will cast your wishes in exchange for your offerings. Hecate also loved black feathers – we can leave these as thanks and to symbolize you and your loved one. Cloves are used for protection, manifestation and spell enhancement and the mirror magnifies the energy, so stare deeply as you chant your magickal words.

MAGICKAL CORRESPONDENCES

- 2 red tealights
- Lighter
- Cloves
- 2 red roses
- Mirror
- 2 black feathers

Light the tealights and sprinkle some cloves in the wax. Place the roses in front of the tealights and take the mirror in your hands. Hold it in front of you as you chant the following words, saying them three times over.

Hail Hecate, I invoke thee,
From the heavens above to the depths of the sea,
To bring me a love close to me.
I cast this spell, so mote it be.

Allow the tealights to burn, and once they are extinguished take them to a crossroads you are drawn to. Leave them there as an offering to Hecate, along with the roses from your work and the two black feathers.

39
COME TO ME

Cast this spell of attraction on the Friday nearest to a full moon. It is used to find new love or to strengthen an existing relationship and works equally well for loyalty, passion and romance.

MAGICKAL CORRESPONDENCES

- Small dropper bottle or sealable glass jar
- Carrier oil (olive or grapeseed)
- Rose oil
- Lavender oil
- Vanilla oil
- Cinnamon stick
- Whole cloves
- Dried basil
- Dried rosemary
- Orange zest
- Red candle in a holder
- Lighter

Pour two teaspoons of carrier oil into the bottle and add two drops of rose oil and one drop each of lavender and vanilla oil. Place the cinnamon stick in the bottle with a sprinkle of cloves. Now add a pinch each of basil, rosemary and orange zest. Give the mixture a good stir and use some of it to anoint the candle, avoiding the wick. Light the candle and, as it burns down, visualize and manifest your heart's desire. If you like, you can etch the name of your intended in the candle before anointing it.

Witchy Tip

The oil is perfect for use in candle magick, spiritual baths, floor washes and oil burners. You can also wear it on your skin to send out energy and vibrations for attraction. Each time you use it, visualize and manifest your heart's desire.

40

TWIN FLAME ATTRACTION

Cast this spell of attraction on a Friday, on a waxing moon phase. Yarrow is a plant of Venus and is therefore used in many love spells to increase their potency.

MAGICKAL CORRESPONDENCES

- Plate
- Dried rose petals
- Dried chamomile
- Dried yarrow
- Extra-virgin olive oil or almond oil
- 2 white candles in holders
- Lighter
- Clear quartz crystal

On the plate, mix a few rose petals with a sprinkle each of chamomile and yarrow. Anoint both candles with a little oil, avoiding the wick, then roll each candle in the petal mix. Light both candles and say the following magickal words three times, with passion:

Hail Hecate, I invoke thee,
From the heavens above to the depths of the sea,
To bring me a love close to me.
I cast this spell, so mote it be.

Allow the candles to burn right down and bury any remaining wax and herbs under a special tree. Place the clear quartz crystal on the top to thank the goddesses.

41

A LOCK OF HAIR

Cast this spell of connection on a Friday, on a waxing moon phase. Using hair in a love spell is thought to create a connection with the individual to whom it belongs. It carries the individual's essence or energy and fosters a form of sympathetic magick. Always approach these practices with respect and positive intentions.

MAGICKAL CORRESPONDENCES

- Incense stick
- Lighter
- 2 red candles in holders
- Small lock of your lover's hair
- Rose petals or dried lavender
- Small red pouch

Cleanse your space with an incense stick to clear the energy. Set your space and light the candles. Place the lock of hair and the rose petals or lavender inside the pouch, being mindful to visualize the desired outcome. Activate the magick with the following words, whispering them into the bag:

Lock of hair,
A love to share,
A love that's pure,
A love that's rare.
So mote it be.

Sleep with the spell bag close by you or under your pillow.

42

JEALOUS LOVER

Cast this spell of harmony on a Friday, on a waning moon phase. Before starting, cast a sacred circle (see page 13). Love is a powerful and positive emotion, but it can also bring out jealousy in a partner. This can be unhealthy and can drive a couple apart. This soothing and enchanting love spell calms negative energy and creates a flow of trust, peace and harmony.

MAGICKAL CORRESPONDENCES

- Small bowl
- Extra-virgin olive oil
- Jasmine oil
- Dried nettles
- Cocktail stick
- Pink candle in a holder
- Lighter

In the small bowl, combine one teaspoon of olive oil with a drop of jasmine oil and some dried nettles. Use the cocktail stick to carve your partner's name into the candle. Anoint the candle, turning it clockwise three times in the oil, and avoiding the wick. Light the candle and say the following magickal words:

Jealousy banished let envy fade,
A love in peace and harmony is made.
Sweet love's warmth is warmly embraced,
Negative energy is erased.

Let the candle burn down, then bury any leftover ingredients and wax deep in the earth in a wood.

43

HEAL A BROKEN HEART

Cast this spell of loss on a dark moon (the night before a new moon). Before starting, cast a sacred circle (see page 13). Dealing with a broken heart is a challenging and personal experience. This spell embraces calm energy to offer a sense of comfort. Visualize a soft pink light surrounding your heart and imagine it slowly healing any emotional wounds and pain you have been carrying; manifest self-love. Allow this light to spread through your entire body, filling you with love.

MAGICKAL CORRESPONDENCES

- Pink candle in a holder
- Lighter

Find a quiet and peaceful space in which you can relax and focus your energy on your healing without being interrupted. Light the candle and sit in front of it. Close your eyes and take deep, soothing breaths to centre yourself. Say the following magickal words:

I release negativity and find peace in my heart.
To the Goddess above,
This is my new start.

The energy is clear, I am balanced and whole,
Fully rejuvenated are my heart and soul.

Sit with these feelings for a few moments, then snuff out the candle and bury it into the earth.

44

ASTROLOGY LOVE

Cast this spell of enchantment on a full moon. In astrology, Friday is connected to Venus, the planet of love, creativity and connection. A full moon brings extreme intense energy, which is perfect for amplifying your spell with its extra potency. One of the best uses of full moon energy is to meditate in its light for clarity on a situation. Our zodiac signs are the heart and core of who we are. By using not only the person's name in this love spell, but also their star sign, you can connect with them on a deeper, cosmic level.

* * *

ZODIAC ASSOCIATIONS

Aries	red	frankincense
Taurus	green	lemongrass
Gemini	yellow	ylang ylang
Cancer	white	eucalyptus
Leo	orange	orange oil
Virgo	pastel green	rosemary
Libra	pink	lavender
Scorpio	black	basil
Sagittarius	purple	black pepper
Capricorn	brown	cinnamon
Aquarius	turquoise	peppermint
Pisces	soft yellow, lavender or blue	grapefruit

MAGICKAL CORRESPONDENCES

- Cocktail stick
- Zodiac candle for each person (see box for colour)
- Small bowl
- Extra-virgin olive oil
- Zodiac oil for each person (see box)
- Brown sugar
- White string
- Lighter
- Plate
- Carnelian crystal

Use the cocktail stick to etch each of your names, in full, on your respective zodiac candles. In the small bowl, blend a tablespoon of olive oil and two drops each of your zodiac oils. Anoint both candles with the oil, working in a clockwise direction and avoiding the wicks. Sprinkle them with sugar. While chanting your spell, tie the two candles together. Light them and allow a little wax to fall onto the plate. Now stand the candles upright in the molten wax. Say the following magickal words with passion.

A cosmic dance our fates conceive,
Through galaxies untold where stars do weave.
Celestial whispers, a love untold,
A tale of love starts to unfold.
So mote it be.

Meditate calmly on your vision in the full moonlight. Once the candles have gone out, bury any remaining wax, along with a carnelian crystal.

45

BRING BACK MY LOVER

Cast this spell of attraction on a full moon. Myrtle has long been used in love magick due to its association with Venus, the goddess of love and beauty. It is believed to attract love and enhance romance and it is also said to protect existing relationships. In a love spell, myrtle is frequently used to decorate candles, enhance love potions and as an ingredient in a bath ritual promoting passion. Witches believe that myrtle can increase self-confidence, making it easier to attract and keep your relationship healthy.

MAGICKAL CORRESPONDENCES

- Branch of myrtle
- 2 red roses
- 1 white rose

On the night of a full moon, nail a branch of myrtle to your front door and leave two red roses outside to welcome love. Chant the following magickal words three times as you place each rose outside:

Oh, great Mother that brightens the night sky,
Hear this spell I cast.

At midnight two hearts will become one,
Together forever at last.
So mote it be.

Allow the myrtle and red roses to remain outside your door until you lover comes home. On their return, bury the remains of all, along with the white rose to represent thanks and new beginnings. If your lover does not return, repeat the spell on the next full moon phase.

46

LOVE ATTRACTION POTION

Cast this spell of attraction on a Monday, which is named after the moon, on a waxing moon to capture its mesmerizing energy. This potion will attract the interest of your beloved.

MAGICKAL CORRESPONDENCES

- Blender
- 1 cup frozen dragon fruit
- ½ cup frozen strawberries
- ½ cup cherries
- ½ red apple
- Handful of red grapes
- 2½ cups water
- 1 tbsp rose water
- Glass
- Rose petals

Place the frozen dragon fruit in the blender with the frozen strawberries, cherries, apple and grapes. Pour in the water and the rose water. Blend on high speed, pour into a glass and decorate with rose petals. Drink your potion, chanting the following magickal words as you sip:

Under the moon's gentle glow and starry night,
I ask to shine with love's sweet light.
Confidence blooms like spring flowers in May,
Attracting hearts that come my way.
With charm and grace
I cast this spell.
I am a magnet drawing love's energies well.
With every word and every glance,
May my allure enhance.
So mote it be.

Repeat this spell once a week, on a Monday, until it has the desired effect.

47

FULL MOON MARRIAGE SPELL

Cast this spell of commitment on a full moon. It will help move your relationship to a deeper level and towards a marriage proposal.

MAGICKAL CORRESPONDENCES

- Red candle in a holder
- Lighter
- 2 cinnamon sticks
- White parchment paper
- Red pen
- Ground cinnamon
- Red ribbon

On the night of a full moon, find a quiet and peaceful place outdoors where you will not be disturbed and where you can connect with the energy of the moon. Light the candle and place it in front of you, creating a calm and sacred space. Take a few deep breaths, allowing yourself to relax and focus on your intention to strengthen the loving connection between you and your partner.

Next, take the cinnamon sticks and hold them in your hands. Feel their warmth and visualize the love you share with your partner growing stronger. Envision happiness, joy and the commitment of a blessed marriage. Now, using the pen and paper, write down your heartfelt wishes and intentions for your relationship. Be specific and positive, focusing on the love, trust and happiness that you desire in your future marriage. When you've finished writing, gently fold the paper three times towards you and place it near the lit candle. Sprinkle ground cinnamon over the paper, allowing its scent to fill the night air. Say the following magickal words:

Under this full moon's glow,
Let love's flame blow
Vows of commitment
As we stand hand in hand,
Bound by love that will forever expand.
So mote it be.

Now write each name on a cinnamon stick and use the ribbon to tie the sticks together, repeating the words of the spell three more times as you do so. For each repeat, tie a knot in the ribbon so that you have three knots in all. Place the cinnamon sticks under your pillow.

Sit quietly for a few moments, feeling the energy of the spell, and thank the moon goddess for the love you have and the love that is yet to come. When you feel ready, snuff out the candle, signalling the end of the spell. Bury the paper outside or keep it safely in a special place until your spell has come true.

48

SHOOTING STAR

Cast this spell of attraction on a Friday, on a waxing moon phase. Seeing a shooting star is a truly magickal experience. You will have heard of the saying 'wish upon a star' to turn your dream into reality. Witches work with the celestial realms to harness this truly magickal essence. This spell is best cast outside, under a starry night sky.

MAGICKAL CORRESPONDENCES

- White paper
- Silver pen
- Heatproof dish
- Lighter

Write your name and date of birth on a piece of paper. Underneath your name, state exactly what type of love you wish to attract. Burn the paper in the heatproof dish and say the following magickal words as it burns.

Beneath the moon's soft spoken heart,
A shooting star spell for a magickal start.
Celestial glow, love is an art,
Forever together, we never shall part.
So mote it be.

When the ashes have burned down and cooled, cup them in your hands and blow them softly to the wind. Your spell is done.

49

BINDING LOVE

Cast this spell of commitment on a full moon. Love-binding spells are a great way of creating a deep and lasting connection between two individuals. It all comes down to your intentions. Cast this spell with pure thoughts from your heart.

MAGICKAL CORRESPONDENCES

- White paper
- Red pen
- Ground cinnamon
- Rose petals
- Jasmine oil
- Silk pouch or envelope

On a small piece of paper, write your initials and the initials of the person you're interested in. Place a pinch each of cinnamon and rose petals on the paper and add a drop of jasmine oil. Fold the paper towards you, while visualizing a loving connection. Say the following magickal words:

In moonlit glow and stars
Above, I cast a spell of love.
Eyes that meet entwined Desire,
Ignite the flames a love entire,

Potions and herbs woven tight,
Bind our hearts day and night.
So mote it be.

Place the paper in a silk pouch or an envelope and keep it under your pillow.

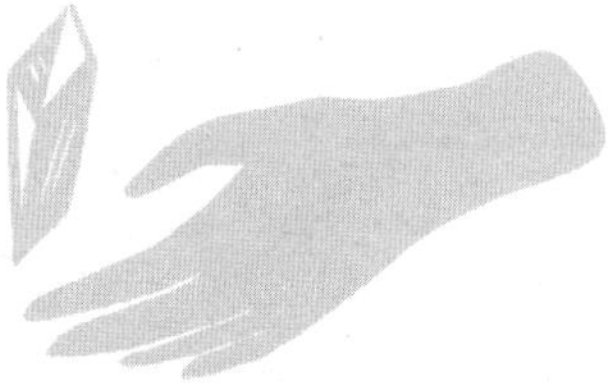

50

WRITTEN IN THE STARS

Cast this spell of attraction on a Friday on a waxing moon phase. Moldavite crystal is a piece of a real star that has landed on Earth. One of the properties of moldavite is its ability to harness celestial connection and intense frequency. Moldavite can stimulate inner transformation and helps unlock the purpose of the soul.

MAGICKAL CORRESPONDENCES

- 2 white candles in holders
- Lighter
- 2 pieces of paper
- Pen
- 2 moldavite crystals

Light the candles. On each piece of paper, write both of your names and draw each of your zodiac signs. Place the pieces of paper under the candle holders. Hold the crystals in your hand and say the following magickal words with the utmost passion:

Stars align in cosmic dance,
Weaving love's enchanting trance,
Celestial threads hearts entwined,
A connection universally designed.
So mote it be.

Allow the candles to burn down and bury any remaining wax with the paper in your garden or a plant pot. Keep crystals next to your bed and hold them for a moment before going to sleep to absorb their cosmic energy.

51

CANDLE MAGICK

Cast this spell of attraction on a Friday (Venus's night), on a waxing moon phase.

MAGICKAL CORRESPONDENCES

- Red candle in a holder
- Lighter
- Red rose petals
- Rose quartz crystal

Concentrate on your reason for casting this spell. Light your candle, focus on the flame and hold the rose petals in your hands. Feel the energy of love flowing through you, then say the following magickal words:

Lady Venus shining bright,
Bring me love for my delight.
Fill my heart with joy and love,
With your power from above.
So mote it be.

Repeat this three times, adding more passion to the words each time. Allow the candle to burn right down and bury any remaining wax with the rose petals and the rose quartz crystal under a rose bush or in a plant pot in your garden. Thank the universe.

spell

NOTES

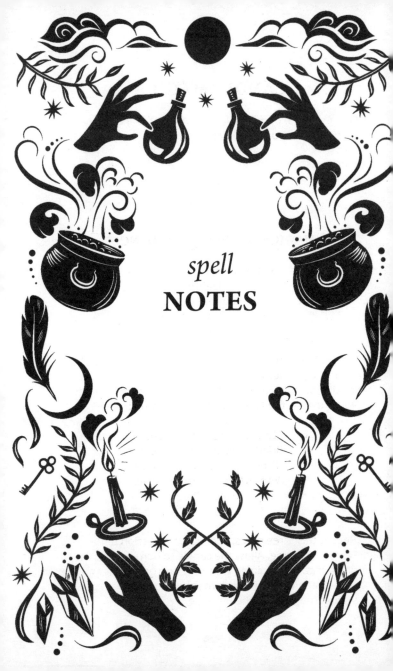

SPELL NOTES

Many witches find it helpful to make notes of their spell–casting, and I recommend recording the details while they are fresh in your mind. It's a useful method to hone your craft by noting the intentions, thoughts, feelings and effects that arise during the process.

Here are a few ideas for details to write down:

- Date/time
- Moon phase
- Weather
- Name of spell and page number
- Intention of the spell
- How you felt before, during and after casting the spell
- Any other notes about what happened around the casting of the spell

The following pages are your sacred space to record your rituals for reflection.

SPELL NOTES

SPELL NOTES

SPELL NOTES

SPELL NOTES

SPELL NOTES

SPELL NOTES

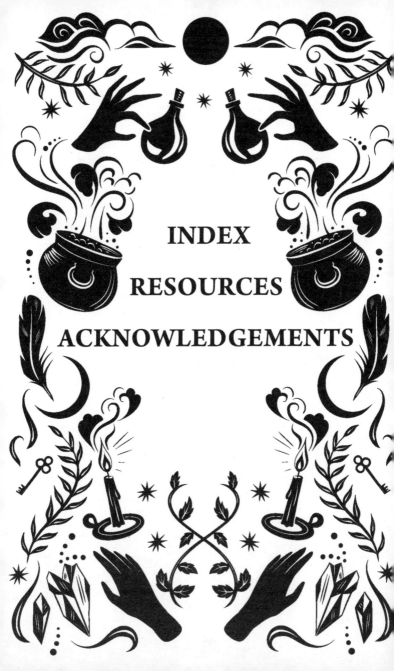

INDEX

RESOURCES

ACKNOWLEDGEMENTS

INDEX

RESOURCES

Starchild
7 High Street
Glastonbury
Somerset
BA6 9DP
www.starchild.co.uk
For herbs, oils, incense and candles

The Goddess and Green Man
17 High Street
Glastonbury
Somerset
BA6 9DP
www.goddessandgreenman.co.uk
For moon calendars, moon and planetary aspect diaries, candle holders and altar tools

The Crystal Healer
Suite F1, Unit 1,
The Verulam Estate
224 London Road
St Albans
Hertfordshire
AL1 1JB
www.thecrystalhealer.co.uk
For crystals that owner Philip Permutt sources himself from all around the world

ABOUT THE AUTHOR

Dee Johnson is a third-degree Wiccan High Priestess and expert spell-crafter. She has been teaching Witchcraft and Wicca for many years, helping others who are drawn to this ancient craft.

@themodern.witch
www.themodernwitch.co.uk

ACKNOWLEDGEMENTS

Thank you to Christopher Falconer, now in spirit, for his knowledge and for inviting me to join the Ashridge Coven. Also to my then coven sisters Christine and Linda and to my then coven brother Paul. They all gave me a tremendous amount of knowledge and time and we shared many meetings in Wendover and had such magickal and mystickal times. I feel blessed to have known them as part of my witch world. In more recent times, thank you to all my coven friends; we have shared so many magickal times.

I believe what is meant for you will never pass you by.